P9-DFA-053

ALL IN A DAY'S WORK

EVE ARNOLD

ALL IN A DAY'S WORK

A WELCOME BOOK

BANTAM BOOKS

NEW YORK, TORONTO, LONDON, SYDNEY, AUCKLAND

JACKET COVER

INNER MONGOLIA Equestrian acrobats rehearsing

FRONTISPIECE

SPAIN Stuffing pimientos into olives

ALL IN A DAY'S WORK

A Bantam Book/December 1989

For information address: Bantam Books.

Library of Congress Cataloging-in-Publication Data

Arnold, Eve.
    All in a days work / Eve Arnold.
      p.   cm.
    "A Welcome book."
    ISBN 0-553-05721-9
    1. Photography—Portraits.   2. Working class—Portraits.
I. Title
TR881.W86A76 1989
779'.2'092—dc20   89-8864
                                              CIP

Published simultaneously in the United States and Canada

Bantam Books are published by Bantam Books, a division
of Bantam Doubleday Dell Publishing Group, Inc. Its
trademark, consisting of the words "Bantam Books"
and the portrayal of a rooster, is Registered in U.S. Patent
and Trademark Office and in other countries. Marca
Registrada. Bantam Books, 666 Fifth Avenue, New York,
New York 10103.

Printed and bound in Japan

0 9 8 7 6 5 4 3 2 1

TO MY GRANDSON MICHAEL WITH LOVE

"...the only thing a man can do

for eight hours a day,

day after day, is work.

You can't eat for eight hours a day

nor drink for eight hours a day,

nor make love for eight hours."

—WILLIAM FAULKNER

For the past thirty-five years I have photographed
people at work—from Zululand to Afghanistan.
During my travels I sought out an endless succession of
jobs and professions, cerebral and physical, to film.
Work for me became an all-consuming subject.
It was natural to the camera—a deep reflection of
the culture and the industrial development of countries
through which I passed. It spoke of primitive skills,
of vanishing crafts and technologies beyond most
people's experience.

In this documentation I could see fragments of our past,
our present, our future. These pictures, born of a
private passion, became a personal cache to enjoy
when I returned from professional assignments. They were
personal work made for my pleasure, without any of the
restrictions that surround work for hire. They became
a kaleidoscope through which to view the way we relate
to our world, the way we work to live and live to work.

EVE ARNOLD, 1989

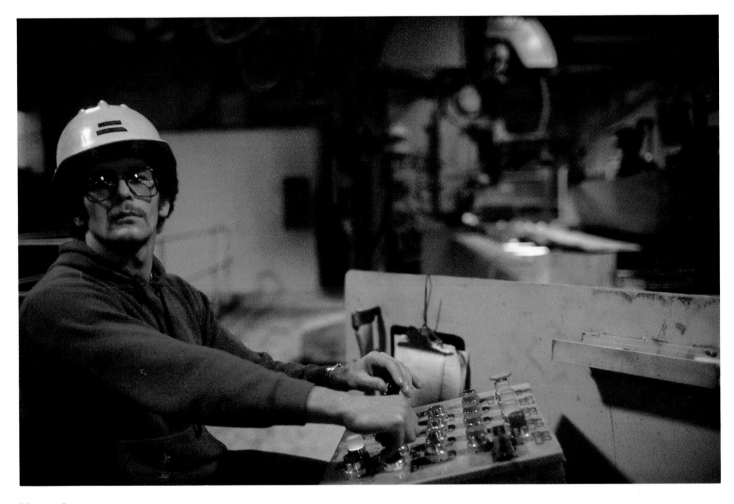

UNITED STATES
Operating a control panel in a lumber mill

SOUTH AFRICA
Gold miner after a grueling day underground

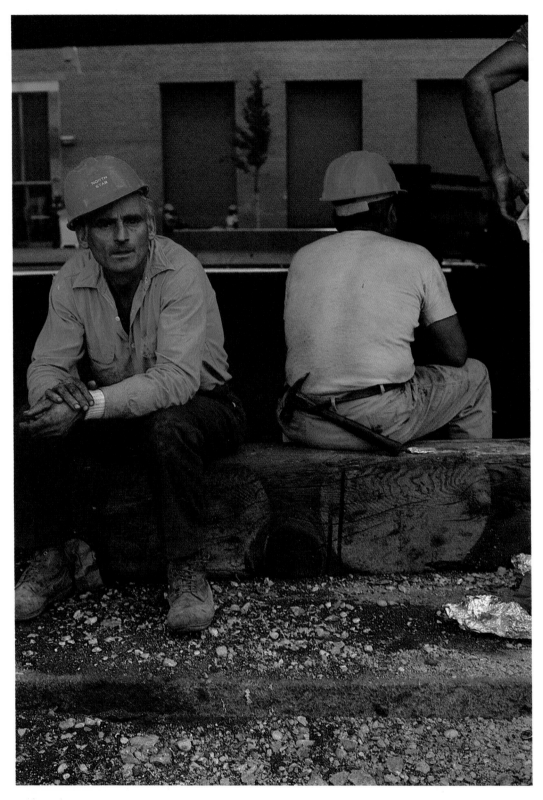

United States
Lunch break on the construction site

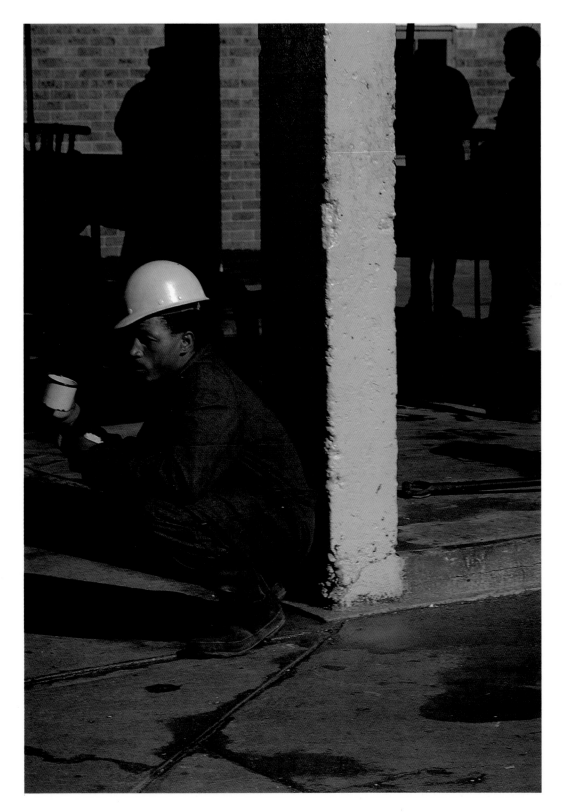

SOUTH AFRICA
Resting at the Val Reef Gold Mines

CANADA
Building a hotel in Toronto

"Why do you work only four days a week?"

Reply: "Because I cannot live on what I make in three."

—BRITISH COAL MINER

ARAN ISLANDS
Carrying a curragh down to the ship that brings
the community's weekly supplies

EGYPT
Along the Nile, women carry home firewood to
cook the evening meal

AFGHANISTAN
Making bricks in the Hindu Kush

UNITED STATES
Building a communal dwelling

"Honest labor bears a lovely face."

—Thomas Dekker

China
Tea picker on the Laotian border

TURKESTAN
The women of the family weave a rug

TIBET
Making shoes

"I tell you, sir, the only safeguard of order and discipline in the modern world is a standardized worker with interchangeable parts."

—Jean Giradoux

Tibet
A construction crew builds a road

Pakistan
Garage mechanics take dents out of fenders

"Which of us—is to do the hard and dirty work for the rest— and for what pay?"

—John Ruskin

India
Breaking rock at a quarry in New Delhi

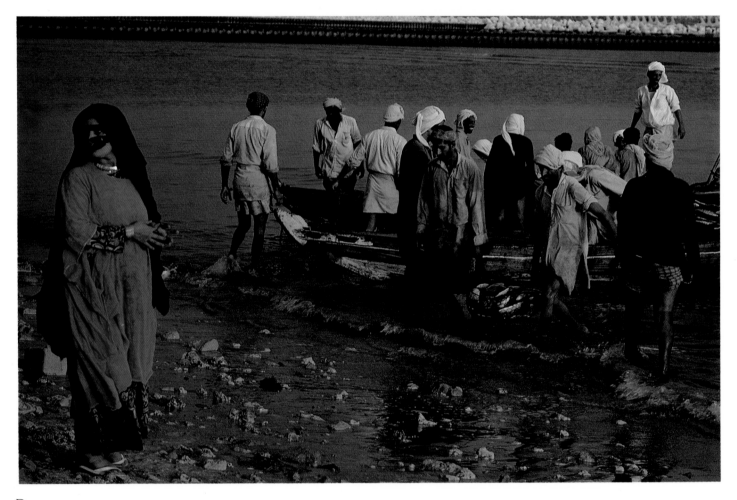

DUBAI
Fishermen bring in the catch for the woman who is their employer

TUNISIA
A sailor

CHINA
Selling steamed bread

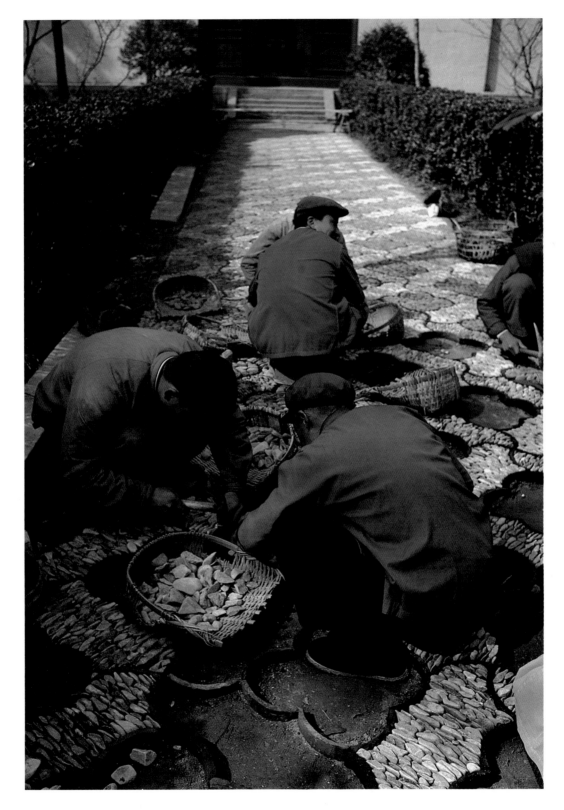

CHINA
Tile setters lay a new entrance to a temple

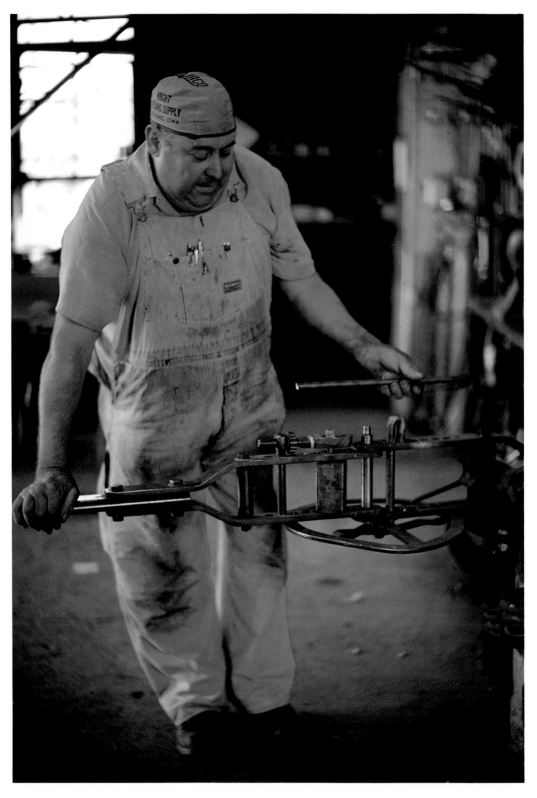

UNITED STATES
A blacksmith making horseshoes by machine

U.S.S.R.
Beekeeper

UNITED STATES
Arranging light and sound for a pop concert

"I felt then and I still feel that the purpose of life must be more than going to work, coming home and going to bed. I don't believe in the work ethic. I don't believe in the rich man, poor man lie about the 'dignity of labor.' There's no more dignity in labor than there is in not working. I never felt ashamed to be out of work: I just felt broke."

—BOB GELDOF, *Is That It?*

"Every man's work, whether it be literature or music or pictures or architecture or anything else, is always a portrait of himself, and the more he tries to conceal himself the more clearly will his character appear in spite of him."

—SAMUEL BUTLER,
The Way of All Flesh

GERMANY
Marcel Marceau miming athletes during the 1972 Olympics

ENGLAND
Lacrosse at a girls' private school

UNITED STATES
Baseball game between the Chicago Cubs and the Atlanta Braves

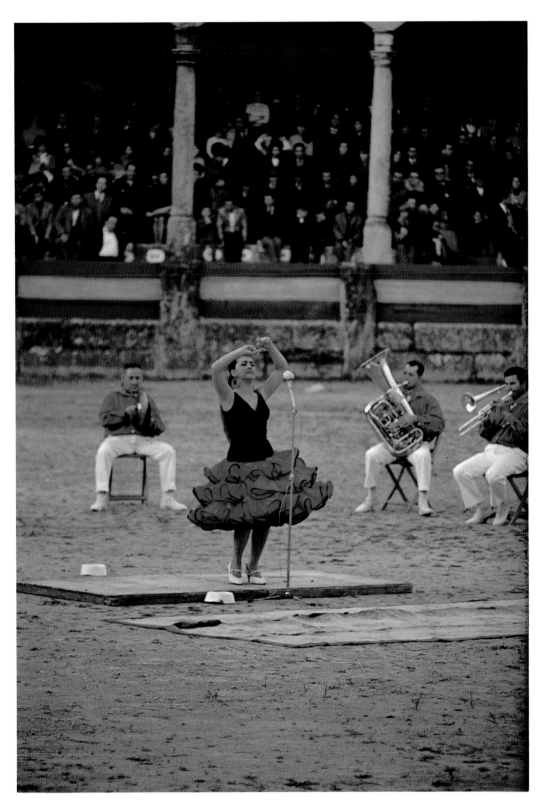

SPAIN
Flamenco dancer and acrobats in the world's oldest-
known bull ring at Ronda

CHINA
Actors making up for an opera performance

SCOTLAND
A clown making up for the circus

ENGLAND
Charles Chaplin sets up a shot during the filming
of *A Countess from Hong Kong*

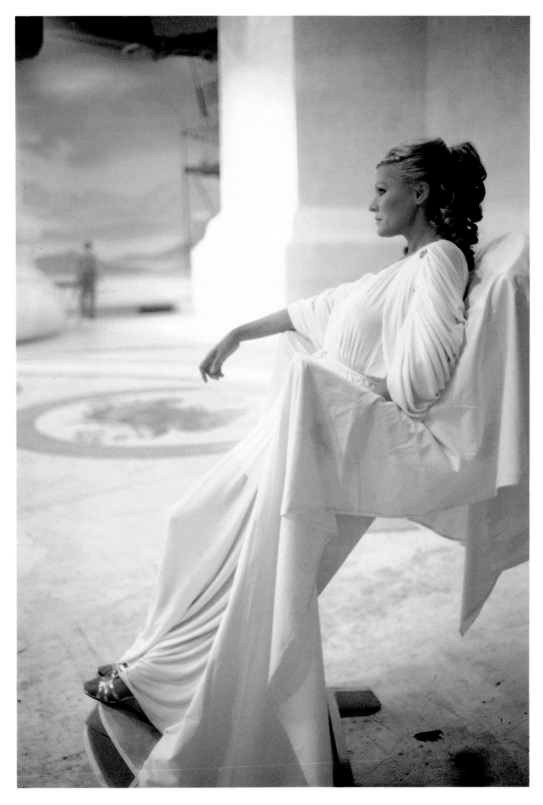

IRELAND
Actress Lesley Ann Down
makes up for the film
The Great Train Robbery

ENGLAND
On the set of *Clash of the Titans*, Ursula Andress
leans against a board to avoid creasing her robe

FINLAND
A BBC crew

PAKISTAN
A street photographer plying his trade

"No man is born into the world whose work

Is not born with him; there is always work,

And tools to work withal, for those who will."

—JAMES RUSSELL LOWELL

FINLAND
A movie soundman between two cars, recording
sound for the film *White Nights*

SPAIN
A camera crew shoots a war scene for *Patton*

UNITED STATES
A prop man on the film *The Flight of the Phoenix*

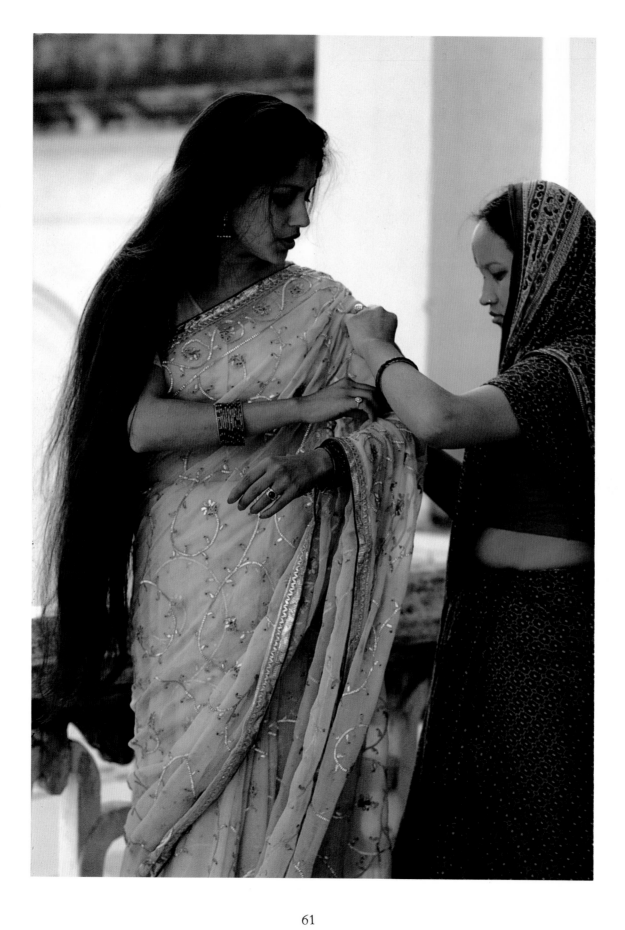

"It is impossible to enjoy idling thoroughly unless one has plenty of work to do."

—Jerome K. Jerome

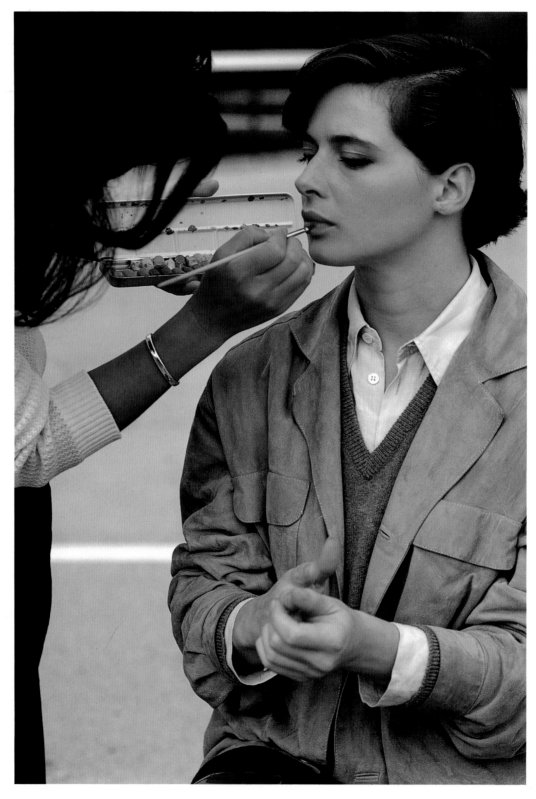

ENGLAND
Models pose for a picture to sell women's hair products

FRANCE
Isabella Rossellini being made up
for a Lancôme advertisement

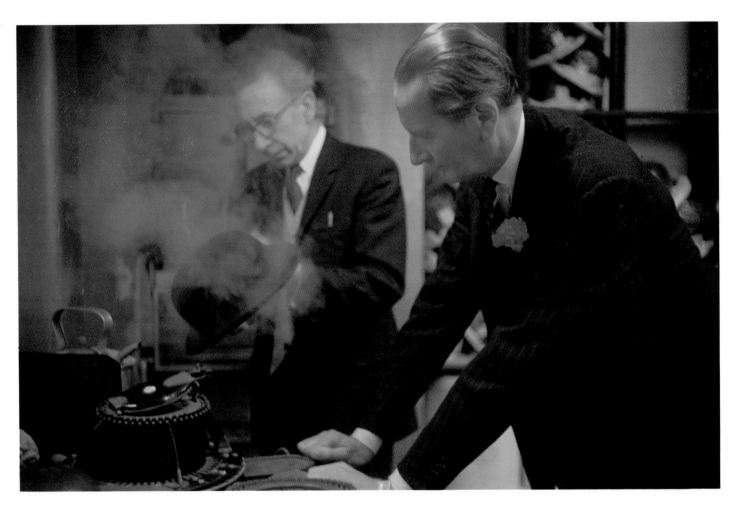

ENGLAND
Blocking a bowler for a "gentleman"

"He that can work is a born king of something."

—Thomas Carlyle

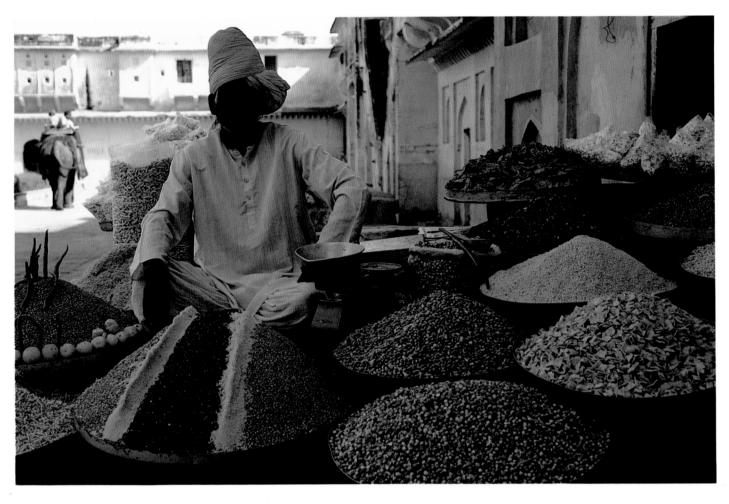

INDIA
Seller of spices and aromatics

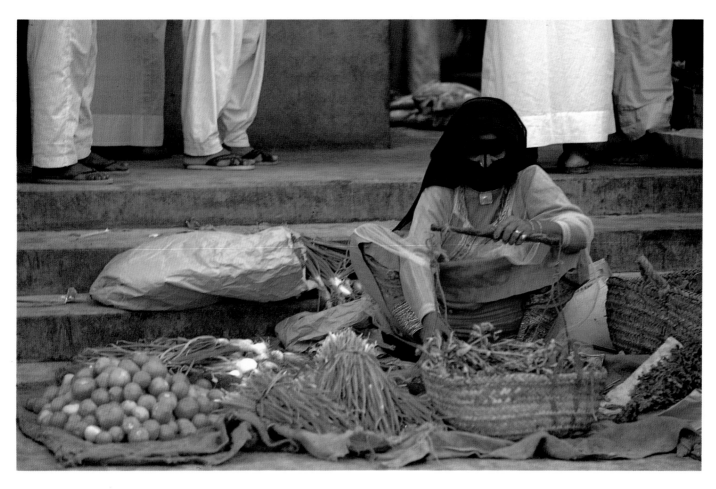

UNITED ARAB EMIRATES
A vegetable seller

"No task, rightly done, is truly private. It is part of the world's work."

—WOODROW WILSON

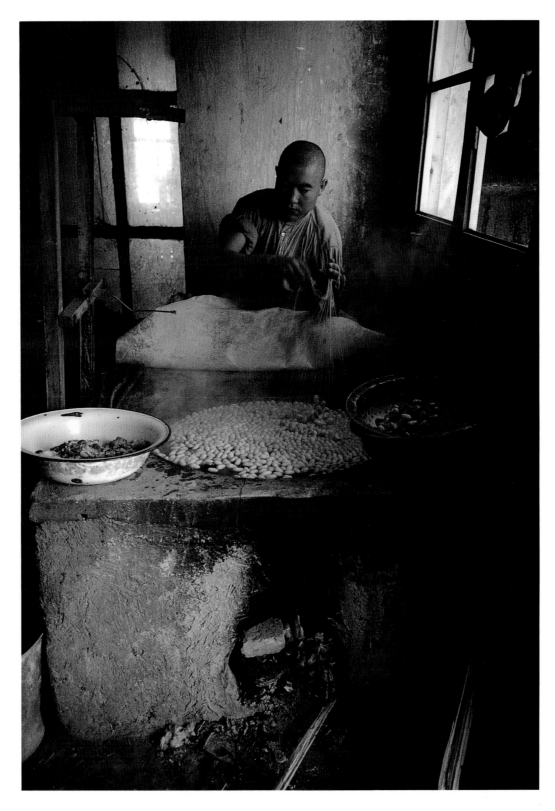

AFGHANISTAN
Removing the strands of silk from heated cocoons

PAKISTAN
Selling potatoes in the marketplace

INDIA
A pepper seller in the market

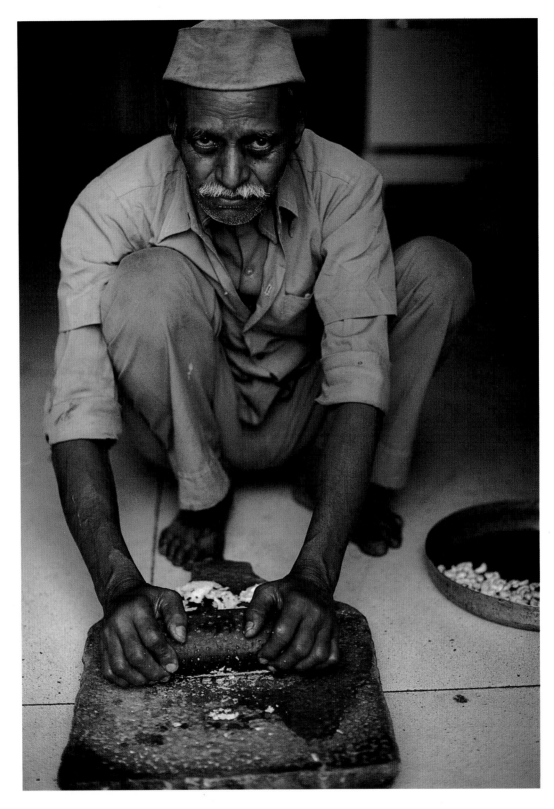

INDIA
Spice blender for curries in the household of the
Maharani of Gwalior

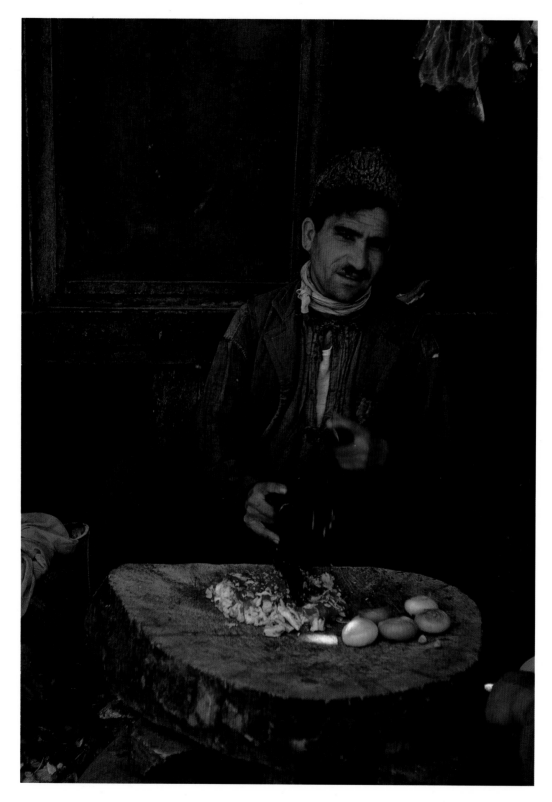

AFGHANISTAN
Hamburger butcher adds an onion to the mixture

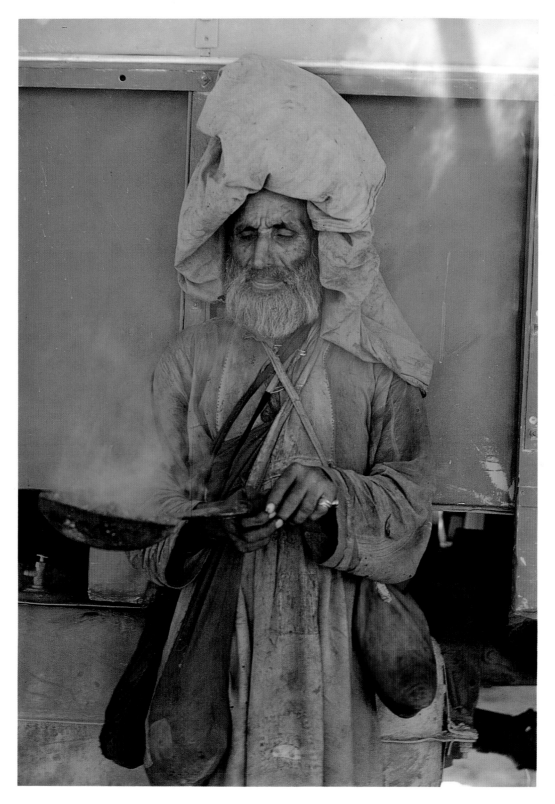

AFGHANISTAN
Every springtime the fumigator goes from house to
house, chasing away evil spirits

"No race can prosper till it learns there is as much dignity in tilling a field as in writing a poem."

—BOOKER T. WASHINGTON

EGYPT
A farmer contemplates his day's work

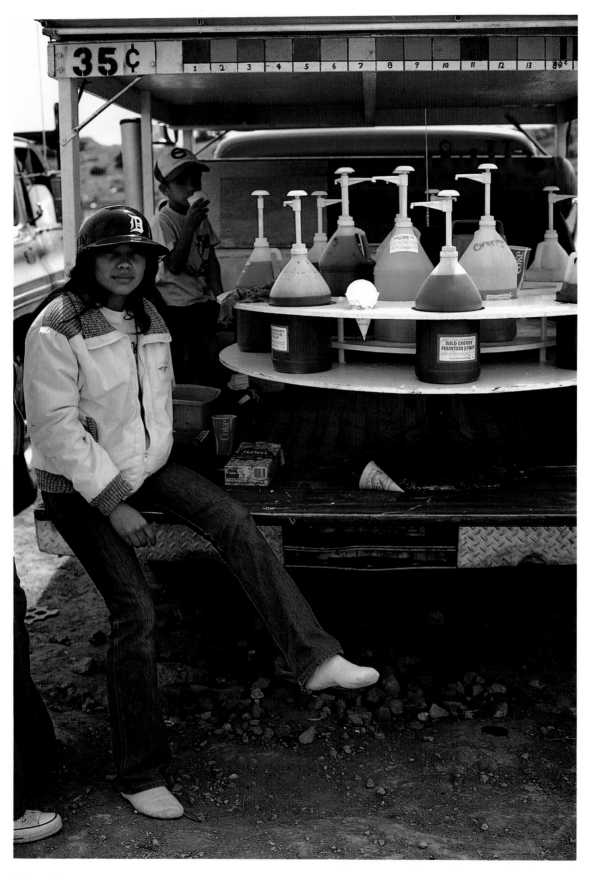

UNITED STATES
Selling syrup over ice shavings on an Indian reservation in New Mexico

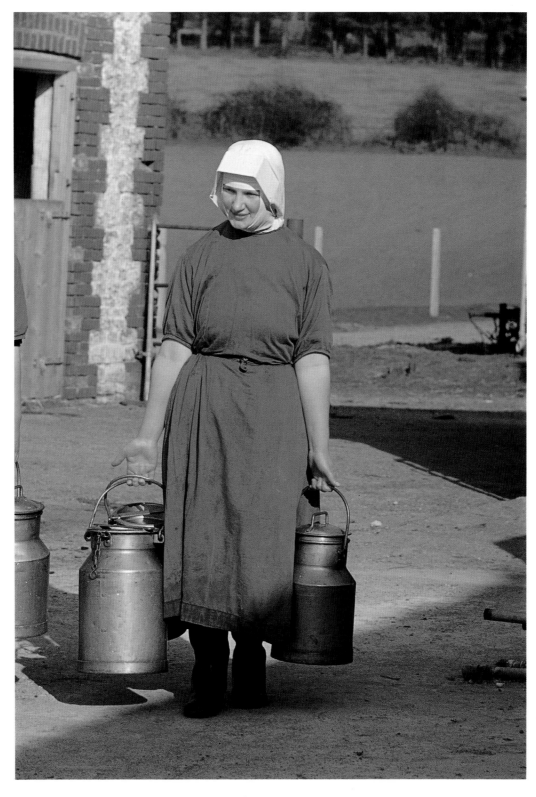

TIBET
Stringing beads

ENGLAND
Novitiate nun as milkmaid

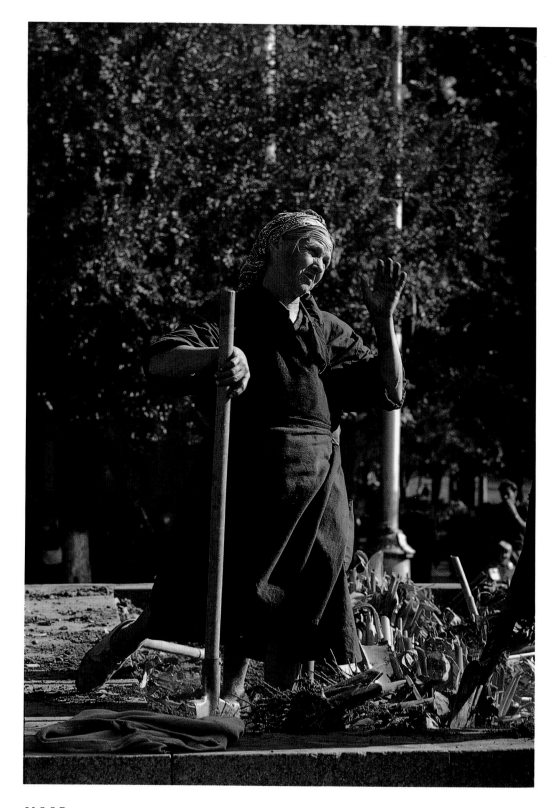

U.S.S.R.
A *babushka* sweeping up the dust of Asia

CHINA
Mixing cement

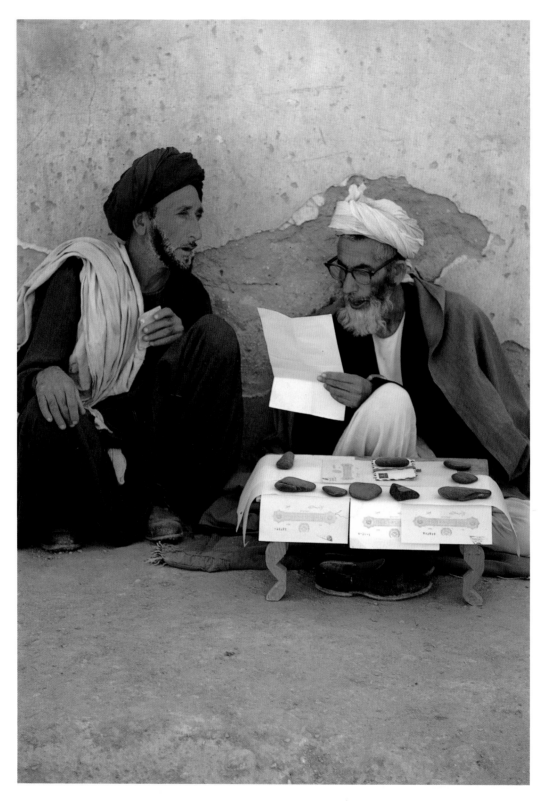

AFGHANISTAN
The village scribe takes dictation from an illiterate
customer

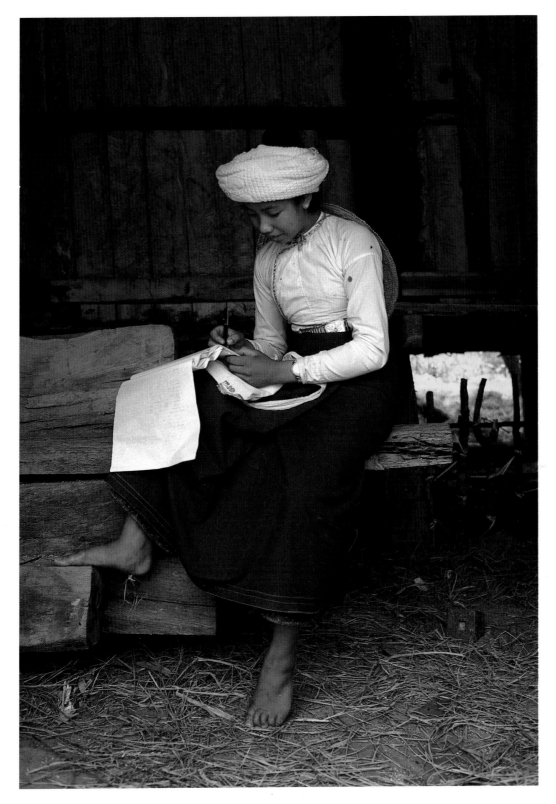

CHINA
Keeping records for the wheat harvest

UNITED STATES
Artists build a communal geodesic-dome studio in the Rockies

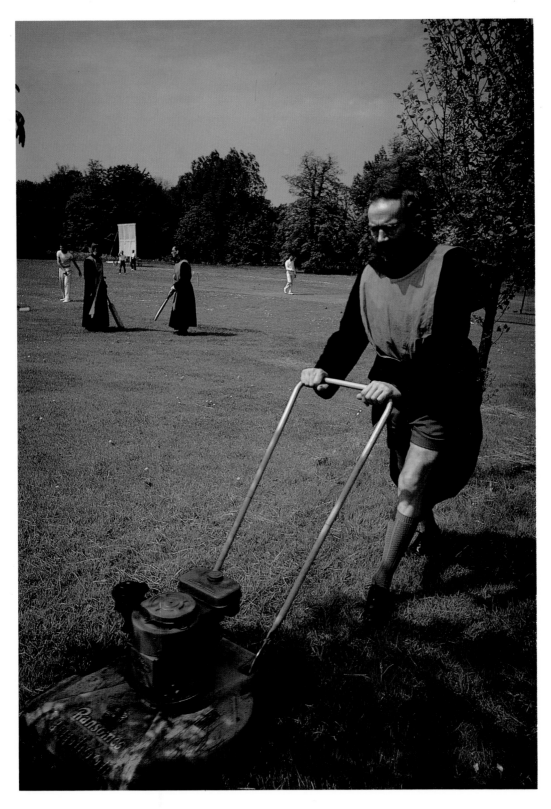

ENGLAND
A monk mows the monastery lawn

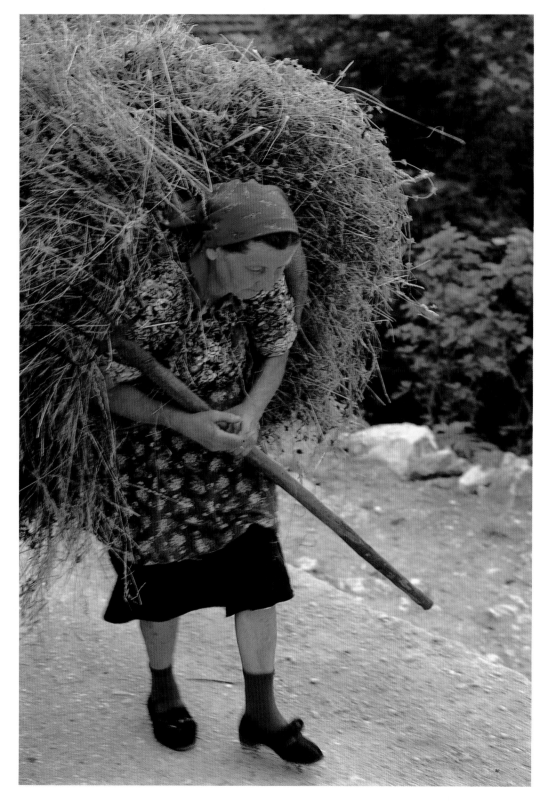

YUGOSLAVIA
A farmer's wife

UNITED STATES
Implements are auctioned at a farm foreclosure in Nebraska

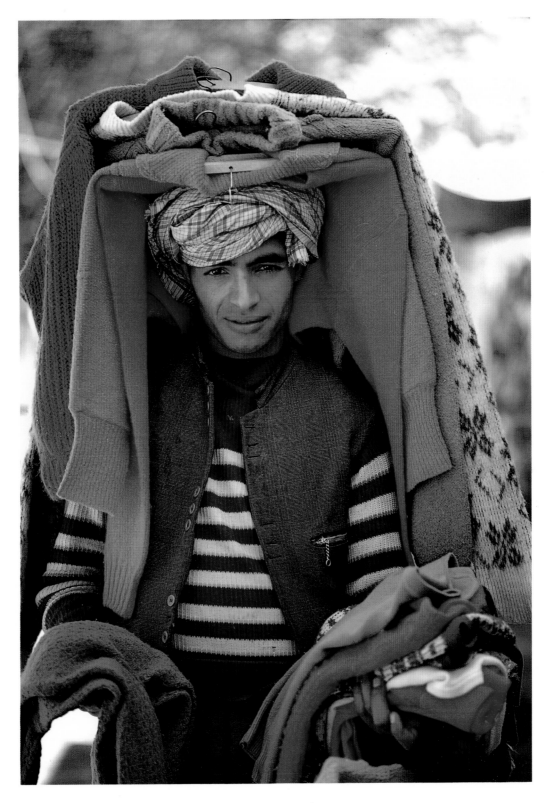

AFGHANISTAN
A peddler carries his wares on his back

INDIA
The local school bus of Gwalior

OVERLEAF: UNITED ARAB EMIRATES
A truckload of new labor recruits from Iran

"Don't condescend to unskilled labor. Try it for half a day first."

—Brooks Atkinson

Afghanistan
Human labor is cheaper than animal labor or machinery

ENGLAND
Kyung Wha Chung before a concert

INDIA
Itinerant musician for hire

ENGLAND
An art student paints a picture for a school exhibition

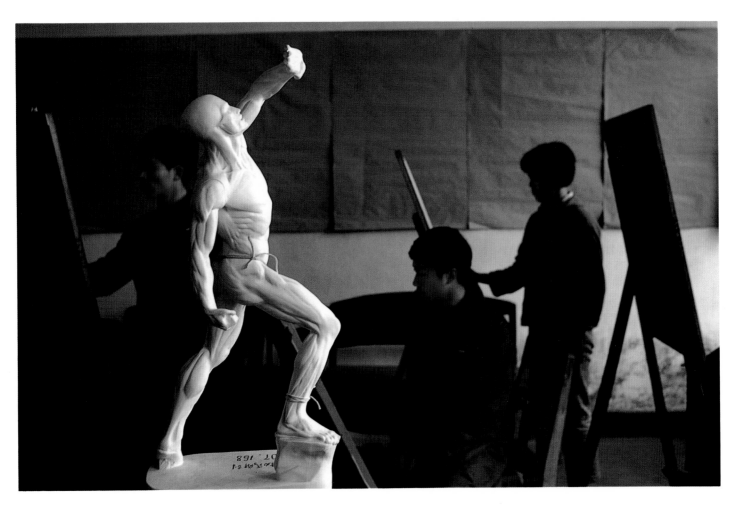

CHINA
A drawing class for trainees in advertising

CHINA
Painting souvenirs

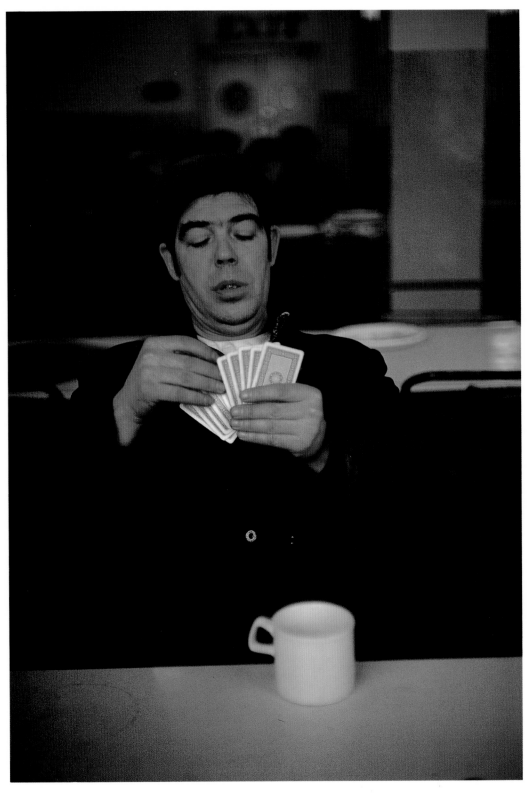

ENGLAND
Lunch break at the workmen's club

ENGLAND
A student in mathematics class at a private girls' school

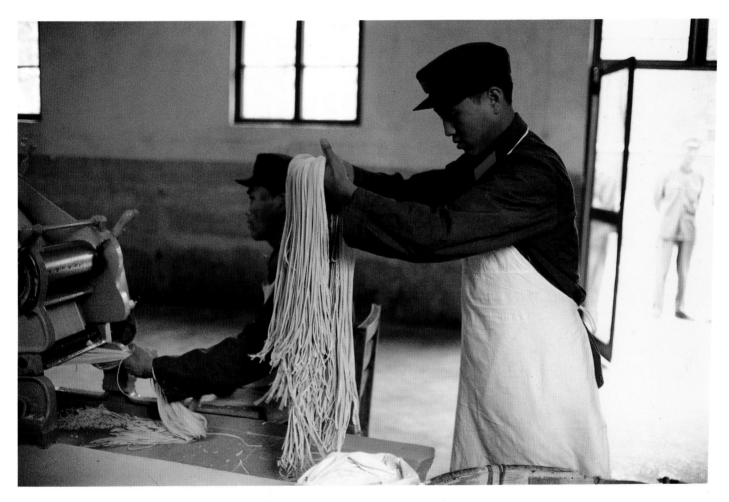

CHINA
A soldier makes noodles for lunch

CHINA
Even the very young help to bring in the harvest

PAKISTAN
Selling tin pots in the *souk*

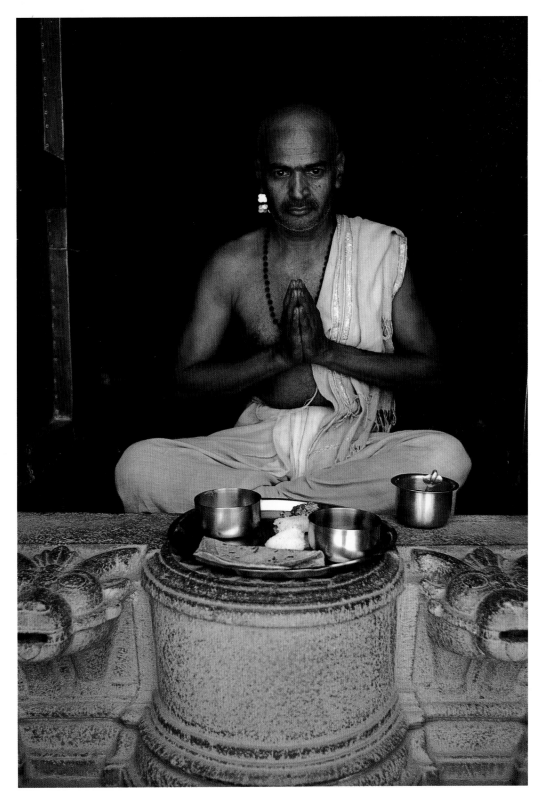

India
A Brahmin priest blesses the food for an ancestor long dead

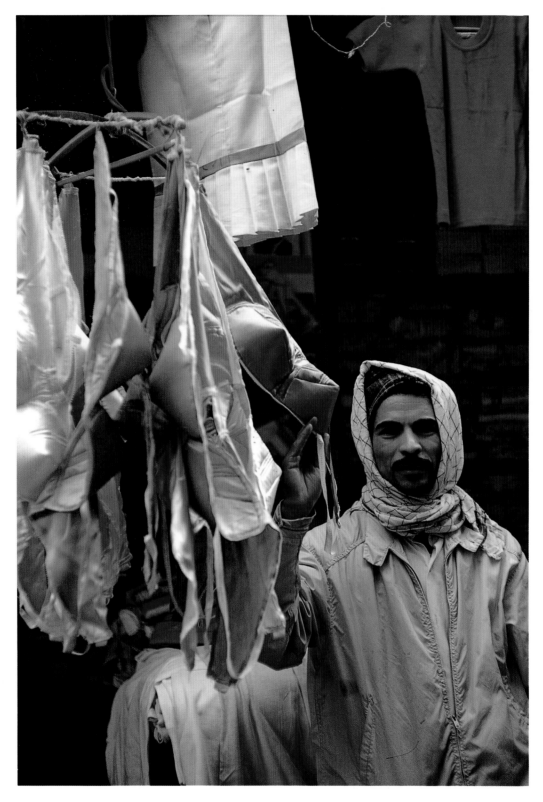

EGYPT
A pushcart vendor peddling his wares

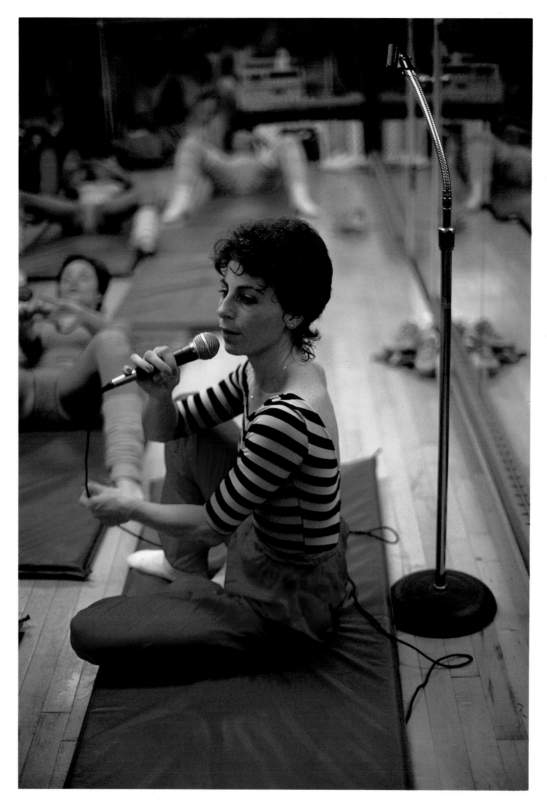

UNITED STATES
An exercise class receives instructions

SOUTH AFRICA
Witch doctor with exorcism doll

United Arab Emirates
Religious drumming for the wedding of the Crown
Prince of Dubai

Afghanistan
Drummers and dancer in the Hindu Kush on their
way to a nomad wedding

113

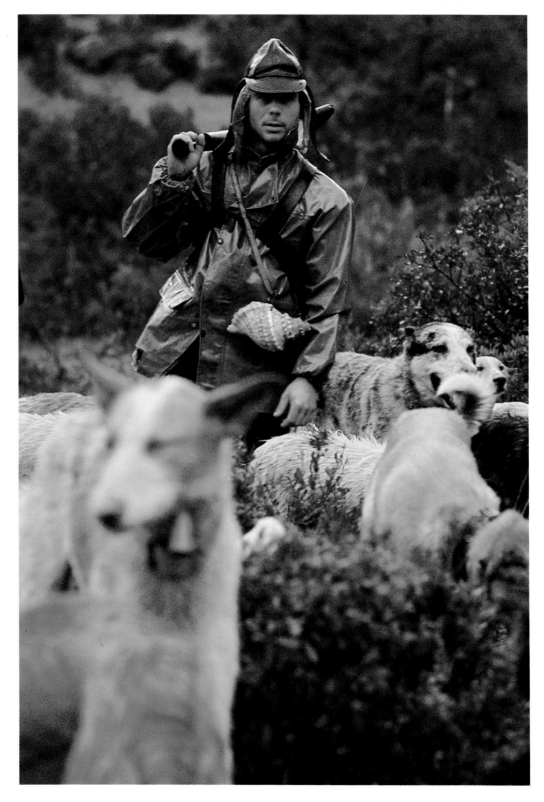

SPAIN
A beater and his dogs on a boar hunt in the Sierra Morena

United States
A dog show, before the judging begins

ENGLAND
Preparing for trooping the colors to celebrate
the Queen's birthday

EGYPT
A hatmaker blocking a fez

117

UNITED STATES
A bomber crew about to take off

UNITED STATES
Sailors at graduation exercises

"I like work; it fascinates me. I can sit and look at it for hours. I love to keep it by me: the idea of getting rid of it nearly breaks my heart."

—Jerome K. Jerome

Germany
Sailors at a lakeside in Munich

ITALY
An Ethiopian priest drumming for a special
mass at the Vatican

U.S.S.R.
Head of a collective farm in the Kuban

INNER MONGOLIA
Target practice in the grasslands

UNITED STATES
A recruiting team for the U.S. Army

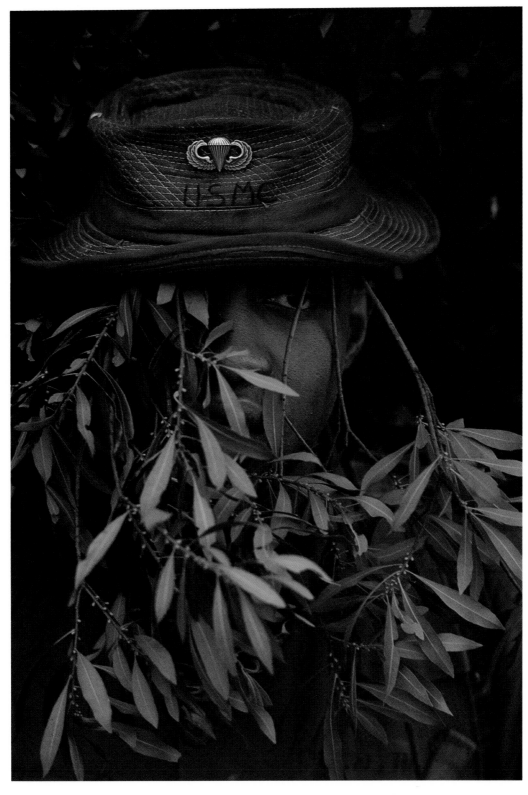

United States
A marine teaches camouflage

United States
Jungle training for marines

"Whether our work is art or science or the daily work of society, it is only the form in which we explore our experience which is different."

—Jacob Bronowski

England
At a surgery run by the Royal Veterinary College, a
sheep is prepared for a hysterectomy

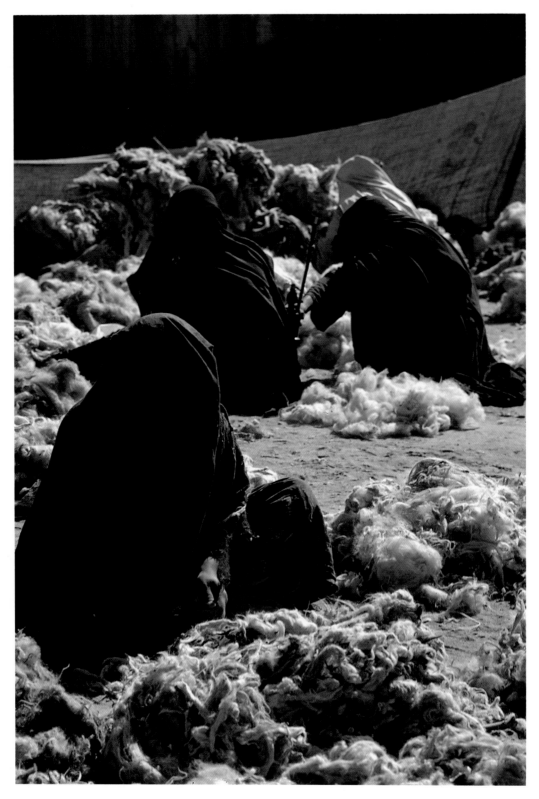

AFGHANISTAN
Women prisoners clean woolen mattress stuffings

China
Spinning silk

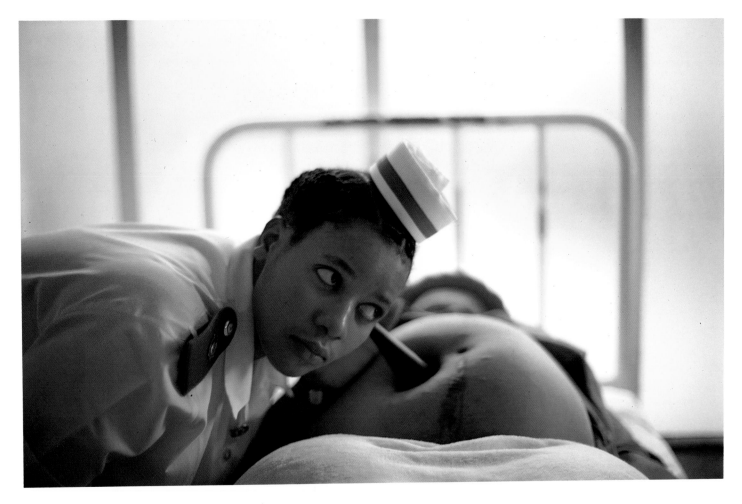

ZULULAND
A nurse listens to a fetal heartbeat

ZULULAND
A nurse listens to a fetal heartbeat

SOUTH AFRICA
Physical examination of a prospective gold miner

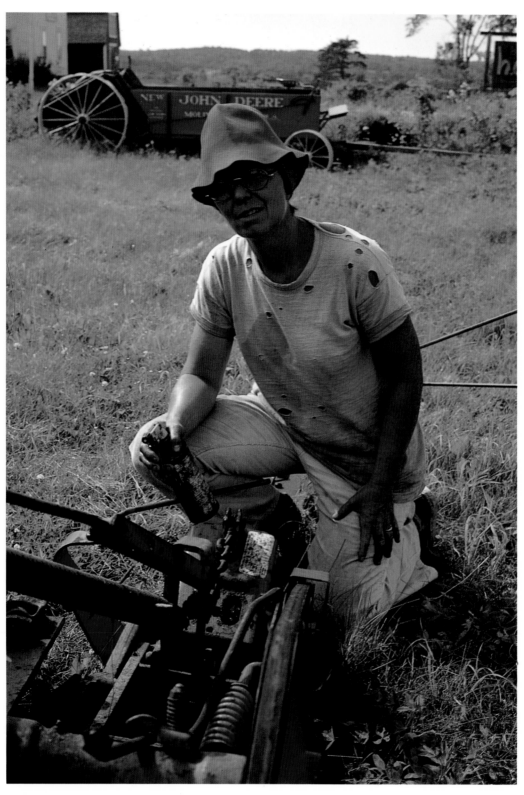

UNITED STATES
A nun doffs her habit to repair the
farm machinery of her order

ENGLAND
A Bride of Christ nun makes her bed

ITALY
Sewing vestments for cardinals
at the Vatican

UNITED STATES
Texas volunteer charity fund-raiser works hard at her donor lists

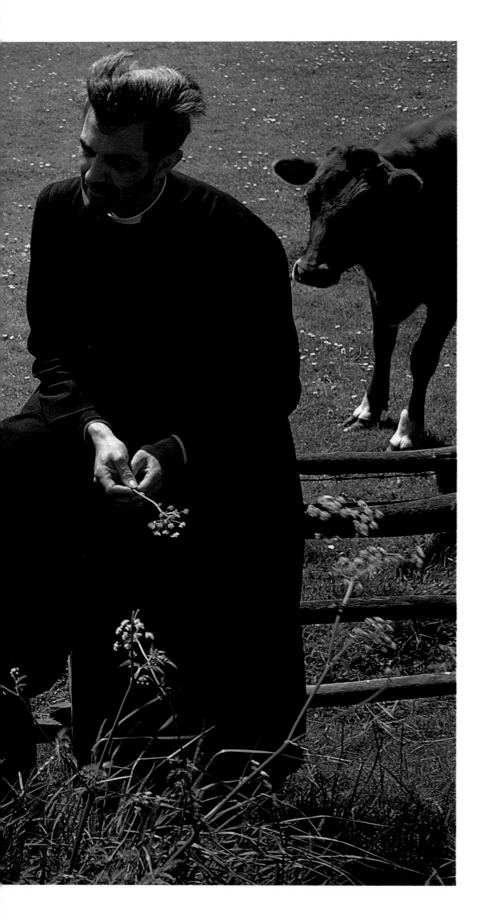

"What is work? and what is not work? are questions that perplex the wisest of men."

—*Bhagavadgita*

ENGLAND
Three vicars from three separate parishes discuss a common problem

AFGHANISTAN
A barber

ENGLAND
A member of the Royal Academy displays his portrait of Queen Elizabeth II

AFGHANISTAN
A beadle in a mosque guards the
footwear of the faithful

INDIA
A rabbi preaching a sermon at an eighteenth-
century Portuguese synagogue in Cochin

145

"Work is not the curse, but drudgery is."

—Henry Ward Beecher

United States
A machine operator in a blue-jean factory

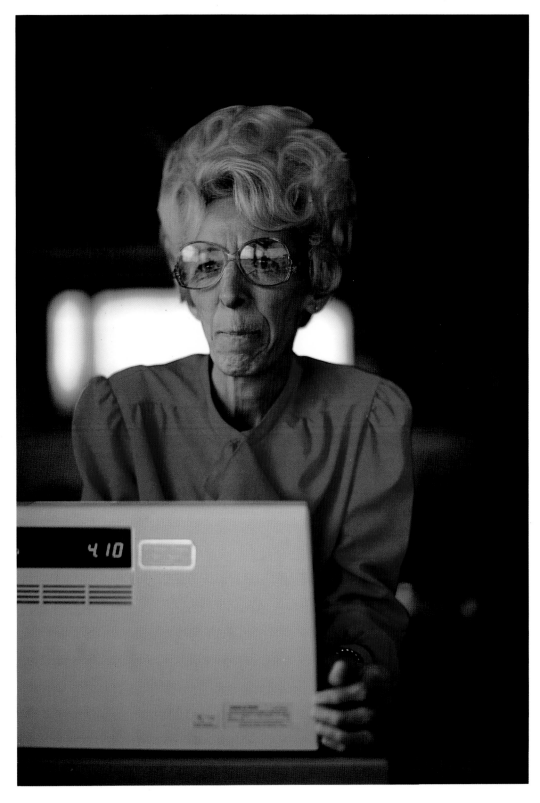

ITALY
Operator on an early computer at the Vatican

UNITED STATES
Cashier in a diner

"Most people spend most of their days doing what they do not want to do in order to earn the right, at times, to do what they may desire."

—JOHN MASON BROWN

AFGHANISTAN
A trio of professional *buzkashi* riders: the game is
played on horseback with a headless goat or calf

Tɪʙᴇᴛ
Herding yaks

United Arab Emirates
Racing camels in Dubai

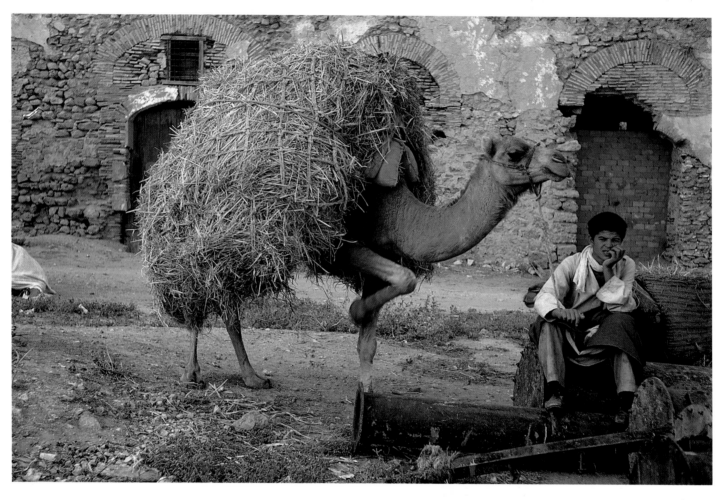

TUNISIA
A camel driver and his animal take a break

U.S.S.R.
One of the oldest men in the world (at age 112)
puts a bridle on a wild horse

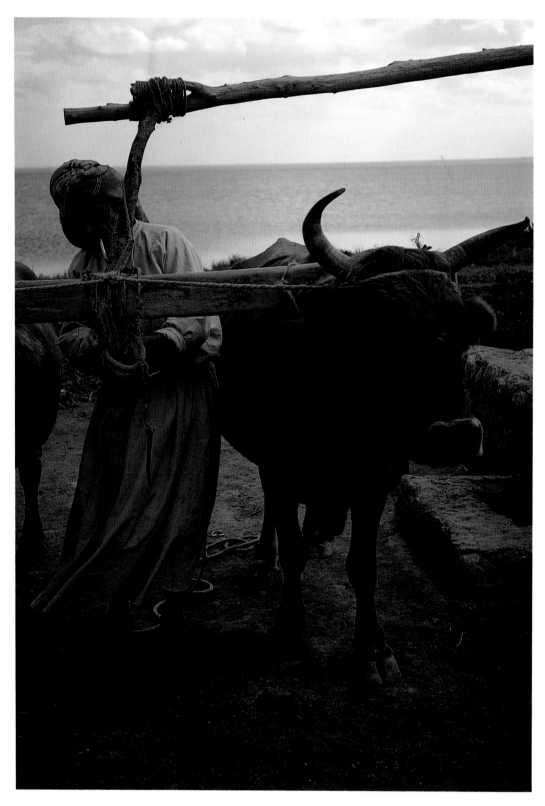

TUNISIA
Drawing water from a well

United States
Polo player prepares her horse for a match

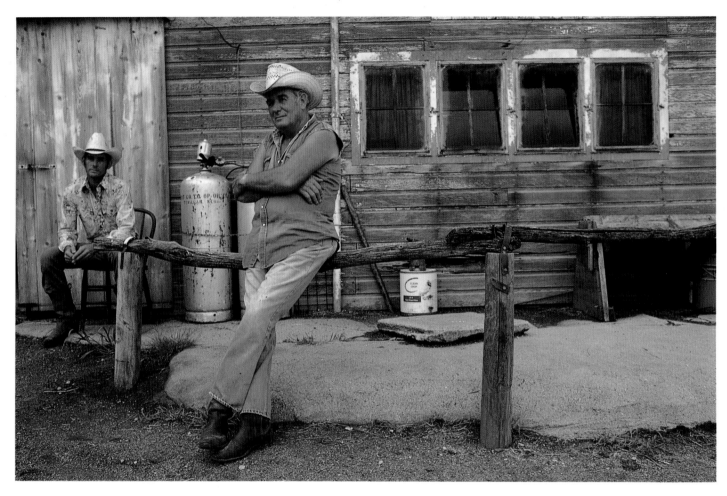

UNITED STATES
A farmer and his son talk crops

UNITED STATES
A ranch owner who specializes in artificial
insemination for cattle

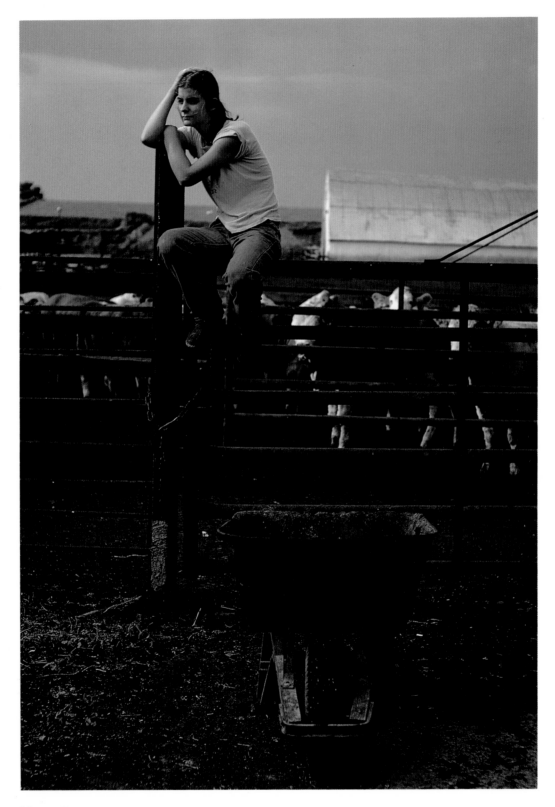

UNITED STATES
A veterinary student with her charges

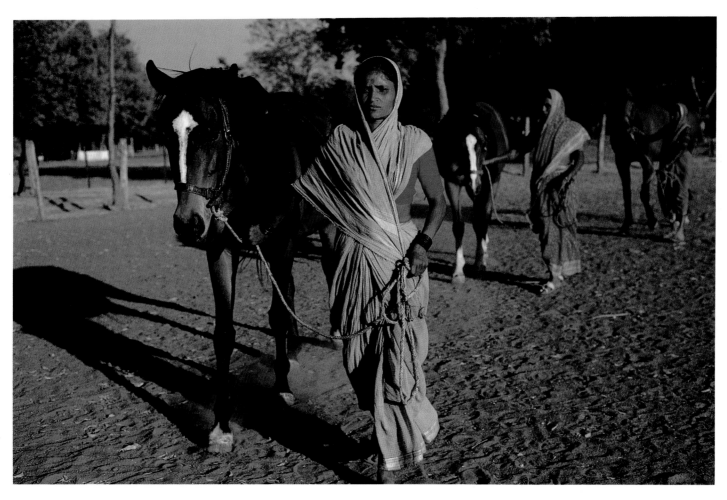

INDIA
Grooms lead their charges toward the stables

"Do your work with your whole heart and you will succeed—there is so little competition."

—ELBERT HUBBARD

INNER MONGOLIA
Equestrian acrobats rehearsing

Text and captions set in Schneidler
Display type set in Bauer Text Initials
by TGA Communications, Inc., New York, New York.

The book was printed on 157 gsm Kanzaki Topkote paper
by Toppan Printing Company, Tokyo, Japan.
Bound in Japan by Toppan.